THE SUN-CENTERED UNIVERSE AND NICOLAUS COPERNICUS

FRED BORTZ

ROSEN PUBLISHING®

New York

Published in 2014 by The Rosen Publishing Group, Inc.
29 East 21st Street, New York, NY 10010

Library of Congress Cataloging-in-Publication Data

Bortz, Fred, 1944–
The sun-centered universe and Nicolaus Copernicus/Fred Bortz.
    pages cm.—(Revolutionary discoveries of scientific pioneers)
Audience: Grades 7–12.
Includes bibliographical references and index.
ISBN 978-1-4777-1801-8 (library binding)
1. Copernicus, Nicolaus, 1473–1543—Juvenile literature. 2. Astronomers—Poland—Biography—Juvenile literature. I. Title.
QB36.C8B77 2014
520.92—dc23
[B]
                                                                2013011621

Manufactured in the United States of America

CPSIA Compliance Information: Batch #W14YA: For further information, contact Rosen Publishing, New York, New York, at 1-800-237-9932.

A portion of the material in this book has been derived from *Copernicus and Modern Astronomy* by Josh Sakolsky.

CONTENTS

INTRODUCTION

Famous children's science author Seymour Simon often tells this story. He received a fan letter with a very complete return address. Following the usual name, street address, city, and state, the young fan added these lines:

> U.S.A., North America, The Earth
> The Solar System, The Milky Way Galaxy,
> The Universe

The return address even had a ZIP code—the symbol for infinity. In the twenty-first century, we find that address amusing but not surprising. We know that we live on one of several planets orbiting the sun. We know that the sun is a typical star, and it is one of a very large number of stars in a star system we call the Milky Way Galaxy. We even know that our galaxy is only one of a huge number of other star systems in the universe.

We know all of these things because we have telescopes and other remarkable tools to look outward into the sky. Before we had those tools, we had simpler instruments. And before those simpler instruments, we had only our eyes and minds to study the heavens.

The following sections tell the story of how we humans began to discover our place in the universe

NICOLAUS COPERNICUS'S REVOLUTIONARY THEORY CHALLENGED THE POWERFUL ROMAN CATHOLIC CHURCH BY DECLARING THAT EARTH IS NEITHER STATIONARY NOR AT THE CENTER OF THE UNIVERSE. INSTEAD, HIS HELIOCENTRIC MODEL OF THE UNIVERSE SET THE SUN AT THE CENTER OF EVERYTHING. HE ARGUED, CORRECTLY, THAT EARTH IS A PLANET THAT ORBITS THE SUN.

and how our ideas changed over many centuries. And they tell the story of one person whose great idea transformed the way people viewed the world and understood the sun, moon, and planets. That person lived in Poland in the fifteenth and sixteenth centuries. His name was Nicolaus Copernicus, and his idea was that the sun was the center of the universe. But wait, you may say. The sun is the center of only our solar system, not the whole universe. You probably even know that it is not even the center of our galaxy. Copernicus's great idea is wrong!

In fact, as you will discover, Copernicus wasn't even the first person to write that the sun was the center of everything. An ancient Greek scholar named Aristarchus of Samos wrote the same thing in a book more than 1,700 years before Copernicus was born. So why do scientists and historians consider Copernicus a scientific pioneer? And why do they call his idea revolutionary?

The answer is that most scholars of Aristarchus's time rejected the idea of a sun-centered universe in favor of the idea that Earth was the center of everything. After all, that fit with their everyday experiences and observations. The heavens seemed to circle Earth every day. Even though the sun, moon, and planets moved through the constellations, their main motions seemed to be around our world. So over the centuries, Aristarchus's ideas were almost forgotten.

Most important, in Europe the authorities of the Catholic Church considered the Earth-centered universe to be God's plan. The church was a very powerful political force as well as a religious one. So a person whose book challenged and eventually changed the church's position truly deserves to be considered a pioneer. And his ideas truly deserve to be called revolutionary—even if they were not completely correct.

BECOMING COPERNICUS

On February 19, 1473, in the Polish town of Toruń (or Thorn in German), Barbara Koppernigk, the daughter of the prominent Watzenrode family, gave birth to a son. She and her husband, Nicolaus Koppernigk, who was a successful merchant, named the child Nicolaus after his father.

The elder Nicolaus had started his career in Kraków, Poland, where he gained a reputation as a trustworthy and effective trader. Sometime in the 1460s, he moved to Toruń and began courting Barbara Watzenrode. Besides Nicolaus, they also had another son and two daughters.

UPBRINGING IN POLAND

Located on the Vistula River, Toruń was a prosperous trading town. The kingdom of Poland at that

TORUŃ, POLAND, WAS HOME TO TWENTY THOUSAND PEOPLE AND WAS A CENTER OF CULTURE AND TRADE WHEN COPERNICUS WAS BORN THERE IN 1473. ONE OF POLAND'S OLDEST CITIES, ITS POPULATION TODAY IS MORE THAN TWO HUNDRED THOUSAND. THE MEDIEVAL PART OF THE CITY WAS DESIGNATED A UNESCO WORLD HERITAGE SITE IN 1997.

time was smaller than today's Polish nation, and many of its inhabitants spoke German instead of Polish as their main language. Toruń, with a population of nearly twenty thousand, was a cultural center with a rich and interesting history. Founded in the late thirteenth century, the town had come to dominate the river trade and was always bustling with merchants.

STARGAZING IN THE TIME OF COPERNICUS

Because the telescope had not yet been invented, the astronomers of Copernicus's time observed only what was visible to the naked eye. They kept records of the objects they saw, as well as the locations of those objects in the sky and how they moved. Their only tools were instruments to measure the angles between themselves and the objects they were observing or the angles between those heavenly bodies. They recorded the positions and the daily and yearly movements of the stars and constellations. They noted how the sun, the moon, and the five known planets—Mercury, Venus, Mars, Jupiter, and Saturn—moved through those constellations.

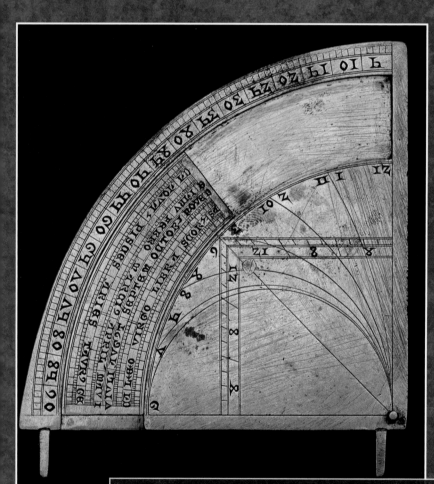

COPERNICUS MAY HAVE USED A BRASS QUADRANT LIKE THIS ONE TO MEASURE THE ANGLES BETWEEN OBJECTS IN THE SKY AND THE HEIGHT OF THOSE OBJECTS ABOVE THE HORIZON. THIS QUADRANT DATES TO THE FOURTEENTH CENTURY AND IS ABOUT 4.8 INCHES (12.2 CENTIMETERS) ON A SIDE. OBSERVERS USED THE SLIDING SECTION TO ALIGN WITH THE OBJECTS THEY WERE STUDYING.

Besides taking measurements, they also used the work of scholars to develop an understanding of what they saw. They used mathematical techniques that had come down to them from the writings of the ancient Greeks. These were further developed and preserved by generations of Christian monks and Islamic scholars. An important part of their scholarship was to find and publish lost works.

A major goal of astronomy at the time was to refine the system of planetary motion devised by the Greek-Roman astronomer Ptolemy, who lived in Egypt during the first and second centuries. That system identified Earth as the center of the universe and placed the sun, moon, planets, and stars on a complicated set of interconnected spheres that rotated around it.

Astronomers believed their combination of scholarship and observation would reveal the inner workings of Ptolemy's system. Copernicus looked forward to being part of that great effort. Instead, his great achievement turned out to be replacing that system with something quite different.

The city had seen its share of turmoil and strife. At the time, Toruń was under the influence of the Order of Teutonic Knights, a powerful group of soldiers who controlled most of the land around the town. For years, the leaders of the order sought to take Toruń from the king of Poland and rule it for themselves. Toruń's leaders eventually formed a coalition, or organization, with other nearby towns in the same situation to keep out the Order of Teutonic Knights. About ten years before the young Nicolaus's birth, this coalition succeeded, and the Teutonic Knights were forced to leave these towns alone.

As a young boy with newfound freedom, Nicolaus probably had many opportunities to wander the streets of Toruń and enjoy the various cultures and people who flocked to his city. Since Toruń is a port city, Nicolaus would have heard sailors and merchants talking of their travels. These tales may have awakened in him a desire to see the world outside his native land.

At age ten, Nicolaus's father died of unknown causes. Fortunately, his uncle, Lukasz Watzenrode, watched over young Nicolaus. Watzenrode was an important man in the Catholic Church and would later become bishop of Warmia in 1489. Watzenrode made sure that Nicolaus was able to get an education, most likely at an academically rigorous grammar school located in the neighboring town of Chełmno. It was here that he probably began his studies in Latin. At the time, Latin was the international language of scholars and educated people. Watzenrode's early willingness to take responsibility for his nephew's education would blossom into lifelong patronage, providing help and vital economic support for Nicolaus.

FROM STUDENT TO SCHOLAR

After years of primary schooling that increased his appetite for additional learning, Nicolaus enrolled in the

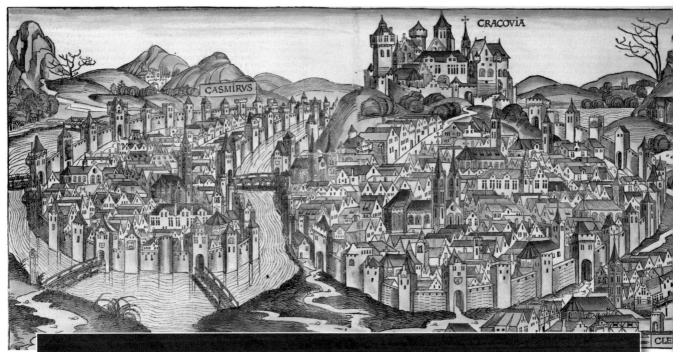

THIS WOODCUT BY HARTMANN SCHEDEL (1440–1514) SHOWS A VIEW OF THE CITY OF KRAKÓW IN 1493, WHEN COPERNICUS WAS A STUDENT AT THE UNIVERSITY THERE, ARGUABLY THE FINEST INSTITUTION OF HIGHER LEARNING IN EASTERN EUROPE. BECAUSE LATIN WAS THE LANGUAGE OF SCHOLARS, HE CHANGED HIS NAME, KOPPERNIGK, TO ITS LATINIZED FORM, COPERNICUS.

University of Kraków at the age of nineteen. Located in the capital of the Polish kingdom, this was arguably the finest institution of higher education in all of eastern Europe. The university had an especially strong reputation among scholars as a seat of mathematical and astronomical learning. Kraków was a bustling city, home to an international community of merchants, students, teachers, and scholars. A buzz of various languages filled its streets.

Young Nicolaus enjoyed the city's cosmopolitan atmosphere. And since Latin was the language of scholarship, he Latinized his family name to

Copernicus, which he proceeded to make very famous indeed.

Though no detailed records of Copernicus's coursework exist, it is certain that he learned from many of Europe's greatest scholars of mathematics and astronomy. His teachers may well have included Wojciech of Brudzewo, a highly learned man who was a professor at Kraków. Wojciech not only gave lectures at the university but also taught in private settings, where he was able to work closely with his more talented pupils.

By this time, Nicolaus's mind was already turning toward the heavens. While he was at Kraków, he purchased and had bound together two important astronomy books. One book, complete with Copernicus's signature on the cover page, still exists today in a library in Sweden. It contains the second printed edition of the *Alfonsine Tables* and the *Tables of Directions*. Both of these were fundamental texts used by astronomers at this time. The *Alfonsine Tables* were named for King Alfonso X of Castille, Spain, who had them published in the late thirteenth century. The book was full of astronomical observations that could be used for further calculations. It provided the raw information that astronomers needed when working on a problem. The *Tables of Directions* was one of many books written, compiled, and published by Regiomontanus, a prominent astronomer from the generation before Copernicus.

Nicolaus's years at Kraków would have a deep influence on his career. His deep study of mathematics while at the university gave him a foundation that he would use when developing his later theories about the universe. Also, it is very likely that he was taught how to make astronomical observations at this time.

In 1494, Copernicus left Kraków without receiving his degree. He traveled to Frombork, Poland, to take up church duties as canon of the Warmia chapter. He most likely had to leave his studies to defend his right to hold this seat, since two other people had appealed to church authorities that they should hold the post. Bishop Watzenrode probably placed his nephew in the position as a way to secure Copernicus's economic future. The job could have supplied him with guaranteed income, but the young Copernicus did not settle down for long. In 1496, he left Frombork and headed to Italy to get a degree in canon law from the University of Bologna.

That may have been the first time in his life that Copernicus went against what the church leadership may have wanted from him, but it would certainly not be the last.

CHAPTER TWO

THE UNIVERSE BEFORE COPERNICUS

Nicolaus Copernicus lived in a time of changing ideas called the European Renaissance. The invention of the printing press about twenty-five years before his birth was leading to an explosion of new knowledge, which could now spread quickly from one country to another. Ancient texts, which previously spread slowly as hand-copied documents, now became available to scholars everywhere as printed books. Those books would certainly have played a large part in Copernicus's learning about astronomy during his four years in Kraków.

REVIVAL OF ANCIENT PHILOSOPHY

Some of Copernicus's most important sources of astronomical knowledge were probably the writings of the ancient Greek philosophers. Their works had survived a difficult period in European history known as the Middle Ages, largely through the efforts of Christian monks. In the ancient world, philosophers thought about questions of ethics, morals, and politics concerning their societies. These great minds also debated how the world worked, discussing the elements of natural history. They even performed basic science experiments. However, they still mixed religion with their scientific thinking, believing that the stars, planets, and sun represented divine objects.

In the Middle Ages, and later during the Renaissance, the most respected of these ancient philosophers were Plato, Eudoxus, Aristotle, and Ptolemy. While other Greek philosophers also developed theories and ideas regarding the heavens and Earth, they never became popular or widespread enough to displace the thinking of these four. Their thinking shaped the way Renaissance scholars viewed the universe and humanity's place in it.

PLATO'S ORDERLY UNIVERSE

Plato was born in about 427 BCE and died around 348 BCE. He was a great thinker on many diverse subjects, including politics, the role of literature and poetry in society, and, of course, natural history and the composition of the universe. He was the founder of the

THE ANCIENT SCHOLAR PLATO (C. 427–C. 348 BCE) FOUNDED THE ACADEMY OF ATHENS, GREECE, WHERE SCHOLARS GATHERED TO STUDY THE GREAT QUESTIONS OF LIFE AND THE UNIVERSE. HIS IDEAS ABOUT THE MOTION OF THE SUN, MOON, STARS, AND PLANETS AROUND A STATIONARY CENTRAL EARTH, AS WRITTEN IN HIS BOOK THE *TIMEAUS*, INFLUENCED ASTRONOMERS FOR CENTURIES.

Academy, where many great scholars came together to study the great questions of life and the universe.

Plato's ideas on the nature of heavenly bodies influenced astronomers through many centuries, even up to Copernicus's time. His most influential ideas appear in the *Timeaus*, a book about the nature of planetary motion and the origin and structure of the universe. In the *Timeaus*, Plato argued that the universe's orderliness meant that it had to have been created by some unnamed maker.

Unlike most Greeks of his time, Plato supported the idea that the moon does not produce its own light but rather shines by reflecting sunlight. That idea originally came from Anaxagoras, another Greek philosopher who died shortly before Plato's birth. Anaxagoras concluded that lunar eclipses occurred when the earth blocked the sun's light from hitting the moon. In his book *Cratylus*, Plato argued strongly for Anaxagoras's explanation. Plato's strong reputation for rational philosophical thinking made his argument so persuasive that Anaxagoras's idea became accepted.

Plato would go on to develop other ideas that would greatly influence later European astronomers. One of Plato's ideas was that the universe was geocentric, or Earth-centered. Earth did not move, and everything else—the sun, the moon, the planets, and the stars—went around it. Furthermore, Plato believed that heavenly bodies were divine objects, and therefore they must move in a perfect and uniform manner. He

LOST IN THE SHADOWS

Because the moon went through phases but the sun did not, Anaxagoras and Plato, among others, concluded that the moon's light was reflected light from the sun. That meant the moon always had a a dark side and a light side just as Earth has day and night. When the sun and moon were on the same side of Earth, it would be night on the side of the moon that faces Earth. That is when the moon is in its new phase. When the sun and moon are on opposite sides of Earth, the moon is in its full phase and we see its daylight side.

But some people thought that the moon produced its own light in a way that changed as it went through its phases. That seemed possible, except for the unusual times called eclipses. A lunar eclipse (eclipse of the moon) always happens when the moon is full and bright. Gradually, darkness falls across its face until its silver glow becomes a dim, deep red. Usually, but not always, the whole moon is dimmed. Then gradually, the

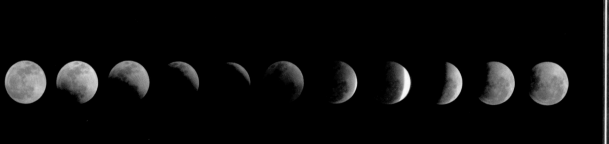

A SERIES OF PHOTOGRAPHS SHOWS HOW THE APPEARANCE OF THE FULL MOON CHANGES DURING A TOTAL ECLIPSE. ANAXAGORAS AND PLATO CORRECTLY EXPLAINED THOSE CHANGES AS DUE TO THE EARTH'S SHADOW, BUT THEY FAILED TO NOTICE THE CURVED EDGE THAT SHOWS THAT THE EARTH IS ROUND.

light returns, sweeping across the moon beginning on the side where the darkness first began.

Both Anaxagoras and Plato thought that the unusual dimming during an eclipse could not be due to the moon itself. It had to be caused by a shadow. And what could possibly cause that shadow? It would have to be Earth. They concluded that as the sun and the moon went around Earth, there would be times that Earth blocked the sunlight that would normally cause the moon to glow. (They believed, incorrectly, that the sun orbited Earth, rather than the other way around.)

To them, the eclipse was proof that the moon glowed in reflected sunlight. Still, while carefully observing an eclipse, Anaxagoras missed an important clue that could answer another age-old question: Was the earth round or flat? Anaxagoras failed to notice that Earth's shadow on the moon was round. That was evidence that Earth itself was round, but he missed it. The answer to the ancient question finally came from the work of Aristotle, Plato's most brilliant student, who noticed that the edge of Earth's moving shadow was curved.

concluded that this movement was a perfectly circular motion at a constant speed.

However, Plato recognized a problem with that idea. The planets appear to speed up and slow down as they move through the constellations of the zodiac. They even occasionally reverse direction in a looping motion before resuming their usual march from east to west. Plato was sure that a mathematical solution could bring this apparent contradiction into line with his description of the universe. The scholars at the Academy would wrestle with this challenge over the coming centuries.

EUDOXUS, ARISTOTLE, AND THE CLOCKWORK UNIVERSE

The Greek mathematician Eudoxus (c. 390–c. 340 BCE), who was a student of Plato's, was the first to develop a mathematical solution that fit Plato's theory of the universe and planetary motion. First, Eudoxus envisioned sets of four spheres, with one set for each of the five known planets (Mercury, Venus, Mars, Jupiter, and Saturn). Each planet sat on the equator of one of the four spheres, which was connected to the second sphere in the set. The second sphere was connected to a third, which was finally connected to a fourth. The fourth sphere for each planet was centered on Earth, and they all turned like the gears of a mechanical clock.

A large sphere, known as the vault of heaven, surrounded all of these. This final sphere contained the stars and rotated so that they also moved from east to west across the sky. The whole point of this bulky construction was to find a structure that agreed both with Plato's geocentric universe and the observed motions of the planets.

To describe the motion of the moon and the sun, Eudoxus needed only three spheres each. Only the motion of the vault of heaven did not need additional spheres. All these groups of spheres rotated around Earth, but none of them were linked to each other. It was complicated, but it matched everything people were observing in the sky. Most important, the heavenly motions were still explained by a set of perfectly circular paths at constant speed.

Aristotle (384–322 BCE), also a student of Plato's, extended Eudoxus's idea. He linked the motion of each set of spheres to the others. He believed that the universe must fit together in a connected system. He looked for a linkage that explained the motion of each part of the system in relation to all the others. Thus, like gears working together in a machine, when the spheres of one planet turned, they had an effect on the motion of the other planets' spheres. To make that work, Aristotle had to add even more spheres, eventually coming up with a universe of fifty-five spheres.

People accepted Aristotle's version of the universe as the authority for many centuries until another philosopher and astronomer, Ptolemy, developed a different mathematical approach.

PTOLEMY

Ptolemy was an Egyptian of Greek descent who lived during the second century CE. While his writings and work influenced the world for centuries, little is known about his life.

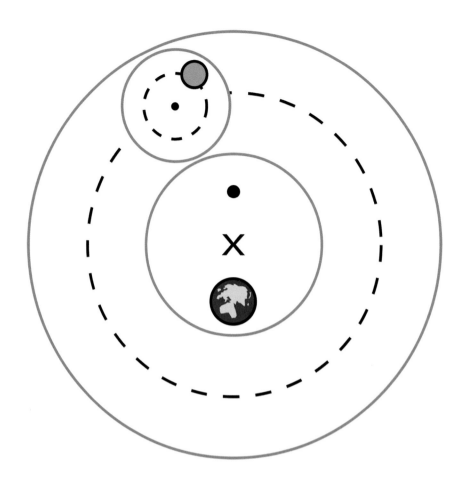

TO EXPLAIN THE MOTION OF A PLANET, SHOWN HERE IN RED, PTOLEMY ADDED THREE MATHEMATICAL ELEMENTS: A POINT CALLED THE EQUANT (THE LARGER BLACK DOT), A CIRCLE CALLED THE DEFERENT (THE LARGER DASHED CIRCLE), AND ANOTHER CIRCLE CALLED AN EPICYCLE (THE SMALLER DASHED CIRCLE). THE DEFERENT IS CENTERED ON THE HALFWAY POINT BETWEEN EARTH AND THE EQUANT, MARKED BY AN X. IN PTOLEMY'S MODEL, THE PLANET TRAVELS ALONG THE EPICYCLE AT A STEADY SPEED, WHILE THE EPICYCLE TRAVELS AROUND THE DEFERENT, ALSO AT A STEADY SPEED. EARTH IS STATIONARY.

Ptolemy's description of the universe had fewer spheres but retained two important principles of Aristotle's version. The motion of heavenly bodies had to be in perfect circles at constant speed, and Earth was at the center of everything. These requirements led to some mathematical complications, which Ptolemy described in an enormous volume titled the *Almagest*. In that book, he added three mathematical elements that brought the planets' motions in line with the idea that heavenly objects must move in perfect circles at constant speeds. Instead of having Earth at the exact center of the planet's circular path, he added a point called the equant.

The sun traveled in a circle around Earth, but its speed on that circle was not constant. Instead, the angle the sun made with the equant changed at a constant rate. The midpoint of the line segment between Earth and the equant was the center of a circle called the deferent. The deferent was the main circular path for each planet. The equant and deferent were still not enough to solve the mismatch between Ptolemy's math and the actual motion. So for each planet, he added a smaller circle called an epicycle that went around a point on the larger circle. That seemed to solve the problem.

But over time, as astronomers gathered more measurements with better tools, Ptolemy's description needed to be modified. The solution was simple to devise, but it made the motion seem even more complicated. They added epicycles to the epicycles. By Copernicus's time, Ptolemy's description had become much more complicated than originally envisioned. But to propose an alternative, Copernicus had to challenge the powerful institution that provided him his livelihood, the Roman Catholic Church.

ARISTARCHUS OF SAMOS AND THE HELIOCENTRIC UNIVERSE

As the church gained more status and power, it became very hard for anyone to challenge the geocentric description of the universe handed down from great thinkers, from Aristotle to Ptolemy. Yet not all ancient scholars had viewed the universe as geocentric. One of the most important thinkers with a different view was Greek mathematician and philosopher Aristarchus of Samos (310–230 BCE).

Building on the work of earlier mathematicians, Aristarchus developed a heliocentric description of the universe. He stated that Earth turned on its own axis as it revolved around a stationary sun. The planets also revolved around the sun. This relationship between Earth and the sun, Aristarchus claimed, produced Earth's day-night cycle and the solar year. His description kept the stars in a fixed place in the heavens, surrounding Earth and the sun.

Although Aristarchus's heliocentric description of the universe was as fully

THIS PAGE IN A 1572 BOOK SHOWS ARISTARCHUS'S DIAGRAM TO CALCULATE THE SIZE AND DISTANCE OF THE SUN AND MOON BASED ON HIS HELIOCENTRIC (SUN-CENTERED) DESCRIPTION OF THE UNIVERSE. SCHOLARS AND RELIGIOUS LEADERS REJECTED THIS DESCRIPTION FOR MORE THAN 1,800 YEARS—UNTIL COPERNICUS'S WRITINGS FINALLY BEGAN TO PERSUADE HIS FELLOW ASTRONOMERS THAT IT WAS SUPERIOR TO A GEOCENTRIC DESCRIPTION.

developed as Aristotle's geocentric one, his ideas gained little support among philosophers and astronomical scholars. By the Middle Ages, Aristarchus's ideas were barely known and largely ignored. But Copernicus was familiar with them.

THE DOMINANCE OF THE CHURCH

By the fifth century CE, Christianity had become the dominant religion in Europe. In many countries, it was the state religion, and church leaders became powerful in political leadership as well. Those leaders found a good deal in Ptolemy's writing that fit with their teachings, especially the idea that everything revolved around Earth. Soon Ptolemy's work found a favored place in Europe.

By the eleventh century, the church had split into two parts, with the Roman Catholic Church becoming particularly powerful in most of Europe. When Copernicus's studies led him to the unmistakable conclusion that the universe was not geocentric but heliocentric—sun-centered—he found himself up against not only Ptolemy's ideas but also one of the most powerful political forces of his time.

FROM PTOLEMY TO THE RENAISSANCE

Even before early Christianity came to dominate Europe, a strong and influential culture had developed in the central Italian city of Rome. Romans conquered the rest of Italy and then created an empire from the rest of Europe and parts of Asia. In fact, Ptolemy wrote while living under the control of the Roman Empire. However, in 476 CE, the Roman Empire collapsed after the last wave of crushing barbarian invasions from Germanic tribes.

With no central government keeping order, western Europe plunged into a period of chaos known as the Middle Ages, which lasted about nine hundred years. Knowledge from the ancient world, such as the astronomical writings of the ancient Greeks, became more difficult to preserve. People who tried to keep this knowledge available included monks living in monasteries, or religious centers, throughout Europe. During the Middle Ages, they copied as many manuscripts as they could find that held the wisdom of the Greeks and Romans. Unfortunately, because of all the turmoil, many works were still lost.

Europe's Middle Ages ended with the dawn of the Renaissance in the late fourteenth century. Italy and France became hotbeds of artistic and intellectual achievement. Fine art and literature emerged from the finest minds in Europe. From these artistic pursuits arose many intellectual challenges, seemingly scrutinizing every belief held over from the Middle Ages. Some great thinkers turned their minds toward politics or discovering new lands. Many others turned toward the sciences and technology, which led to many great inventions, including the compass, gunpowder, and the printing press.

Astronomy, or the study of the heavens, also emerged. With it, people began challenging age-old beliefs. Among them was Nicolaus Copernicus, who challenged the Catholic Church's belief in a geocentric universe. It can easily be said that Copernicus "moved heaven and earth," transforming the way people viewed their place in them.

CHAPTER THREE

CHALLENGING PTOLEMY

Like most young people who went to universities, Copernicus expected to study the knowledge of the great scholars who came before him. Those scholars were revered as sages, and their ideas were viewed as the sources of truth, wisdom, and culture. Challenging them was nearly unthinkable, especially if their ideas had been accepted for centuries. Yet before his student days were over, Copernicus discovered that the best route to new knowledge often involved challenging old knowledge. Becoming a scholar often required questioning and challenging sages and reshaping their ideas.

Copernicus arrived in Bologna sometime late in 1496 and enrolled at the University of Bologna as a student of canon law. This was primarily to please his uncle, Bishop Watzenrode, who

COPERNICUS STUDIED CANON LAW, MATHEMATICS, AND ASTRONOMY AT THE UNIVERSITY OF BOLOGNA, ITALY, BEGINNING IN 1496. COPERNICUS ESPECIALLY ENJOYED THE CITY FOR ITS ARCHITECTURE AND ITS RICH HISTORY, WHICH ARE STILL EVIDENT IN THIS MODERN AERIAL VIEW.

had also earned a degree in canon law. Bologna was a rich and prosperous city with one of Europe's oldest universities. It had many German-speaking students, with whom Copernicus made friends. In 1498, when his older brother Andrew arrived in the city to begin his studies as well, Copernicus had someone with whom to share the wonders of the city and its rich history.

The impressive architecture in Bologna may have also had an influence on Copernicus. The city was home to two great towers, Garisenda and Asinelli, which stood near the campus. These two towers were most likely taller than any he had ever seen before and would have helped continually draw his eyes upward to the heavens as he made his way around the city.

DISCOVERING A NEW PERSPECTIVE

Although canon law was not necessarily Copernicus's first love, his enrollment entitled him to take classes anywhere else in the university that he wished. This allowed him to continue to pursue his interest in astronomy and mathematics. He sought out Domenico Maria da Novara, the university's professor of astronomy, who had begun to publish challenging and original ideas on the subject. For example, in 1489, da Novara published a book declaring that Ptolemy, long considered the foremost authority on Earth's geography, had incorrectly calculated the latitudes of most of Europe's cities. Da Novara concluded that these latitudes were actually up to one degree and ten minutes greater than Ptolemy had suggested in his *Geography* some twelve centuries earlier.

For da Novara this indicated a shift in the direction of the tilt of Earth's axis. Da Novara also concluded that Earth did not stand still but instead rotated on its own axis. Da Novara's exact calculations would eventually be proven wrong, but he was right about Earth's rotation.

The scholar would have a profound impact on Copernicus. Through da Novara's actions, Copernicus learned that it was possible to publicly challenge long-held beliefs, such as those put forth by Ptolemy and supported by the Catholic Church, with a new perspective.

Because students at the university roomed in private lodgings, Copernicus secured a room in professor da Novara's house. This gave him a chance to work more closely with the professor and gain his respect. According to the writings of Copernicus's student Rheticus, Copernicus said his knowledge of astronomy was so strong at this time that da Novara considered him "not so much the pupil as the assistant and witness of the observations."

THIS MODERN PHOTOGRAPH OF A CLASSIC PORTICO CAPTURES THE ATMOSPHERE OF THE UNIVERSITY OF BOLOGNA, WHERE COPERNICUS STUDIED WITH ASTRONOMY PROFESSOR DOMENICO MARIA DA NOVARA. DA NOVARA'S 1489 BOOK SHOWED COPERNICUS THAT SCHOLARS COULD CHALLENGE THE WRITINGS OF EARLIER AUTHORITIES.

AN OBSERVATION THAT CHANGED ASTRONOMY

On the evening of March 9, 1497, Copernicus, along with da Novara, recorded that the moon occulted—or appeared to pass in front of and hide—the star Aldebaran. It was Copernicus's first astronomical observation, and it was contrary to Ptolemy's observation. This proved that Ptolemy was not always correct, despite what other Renaissance scholars and astronomers believed. As Copernicus noted later in his masterwork *De Revolutionibus Orbium Coelestium* ("On the Revolutions of the Heavenly Spheres"), this astronomical observation disproved Ptolemy's belief regarding the distance of the moon from Earth.

This one small observation would have a major impact on the history of the world. It showed that da Novara was correct to question Ptolemy. But it meant far more than that to Copernicus and science. Copernicus realized that by using observation as evidence, he or any other scientist would no longer be bound by tradition when trying to determine the nature of the universe.

MAKING A NAME IN ROME

Eventually, Copernicus lost his financial support, and he and his brother were forced to leave the university before completing their degrees. Many historians speculate that this is why Copernicus left Bologna and moved to Rome. Others claim different reasons for the move. The next year, 1500, was declared a jubilee year by Pope Alexander VI. A jubilee year occurred every fifty years and was marked with special ceremonies

KOPERNIK OBSERVANT, A ROME, UNE ÉCLIPSE DE LUNE

IN 1499, COPERNICUS LEFT BOLOGNA FOR ROME, WHERE HE SOON CAUGHT THE ATTENTION OF THE GREAT SCHOLARS OF HIS TIME. THIS DRAWING SHOWS HIM OBSERVING A LUNAR ECLIPSE THERE IN 1500.

and entertainment. Pilgrims would come from all over Europe to get the special blessings that the pope and Catholic Church provided at these times. Both brothers probably wished to see the spectacle in Rome. No matter the reason, sometime in the fall of 1500, Copernicus arrived in Rome, where he soon caught the attention of the great scholars of the day.

As a twenty-seven-year-old who had come from a cosmopolitan background, Copernicus must have enjoyed all the crowds that came for the jubilee festivals once he arrived in Rome. Home to the Roman Catholic Church, Rome in essence was the capital of Europe, if not the world. The city was a breeding ground of art and ideas. Rome swelled with pilgrims, students, and visitors from around Christian Europe. Copernicus, however, was not so blinded by the celebrations that he forgot his love of astronomy or his desire to further investigate the heavens.

Copernicus quickly established himself as a great mind, impressing both students and peers alike. Rheticus related a story of his teacher in *Narratio Prima* published in 1540: "About the year 1500, being twenty-seven years of age more or less, [Copernicus] lectured on mathematics before a large audience of students and a throng of great men and experts in this branch of knowledge." These impressive lectures were delivered to the general public and likely contained Copernicus's general observations concerning astronomical scholarship.

REDISCOVERING THE ANCIENT GREEKS

Copernicus's studies at the University of Padua included a branch of knowledge that was important for both his astronomical work and his medical training—the learning of ancient Greek. Knowledge of Greek allowed Copernicus to examine the sources of the ancient philosophers in their original language. Here, he had the opportunity to clear up any misunderstandings that had crept in through the various translations that had been passed down over the centuries. By comparing the original ancient Greek writings to new translations, Copernicus documented mistakes in the translated versions. He needed to have the correct information on which to base his own work.

Did Copernicus discover the writings of Aristarchus at Padua? Perhaps, but whether it was then or later, his willingness to challenge well-established ideas, even those of Ptolemy, would guide his scholarship for the rest of his life.

AT THE UNIVERSITY OF PADUA, COPERNICUS STUDIED HAND COPIES OF ANCIENT GREEK MANUSCRIPTS, SUCH AS THIS ONE ABOUT THE HEAVENS BY ARISTOTLE.

His lectures at this time probably did not theorize on the heliocentric nature of the universe. From the preserved writings of other astronomers that attended the 1500 jubilee, there is no mention of anything about a young man expounding on a sun-centered universe. The idea of heliocentricity would have been a bombshell to them, so it is likely that Copernicus had not yet devised his earth-shaking theory. Still, his lectures doubtless earned him respect with the experts in his field. They were also a way for him to keep his focus on learning despite all the distractions in the city.

Meanwhile, Copernicus continued to make astronomical observations. On November 6, 1500, he recorded a lunar eclipse. These first-recorded observations would eventually become pieces of a larger body of work. His early observations would help piece together one of the largest mysteries in the universe.

STUDIES IN PADUA AND FERRARA

The following year, Copernicus and his brother Andrew went to Padua while on a leave of absence from their duties as canons in Frombork. Copernicus chose Padua for a practical reason—his desire to continue his leave of absence and his studying. Since the canons did not have any staff with medical training to care for them if they got sick or as they aged, Copernicus told them that he wanted to learn medicine. The church granted his request, since the University of Padua was a widely respected school of medicine.

However, Copernicus only asked for a two-year extension on his leave of absence even though a medical degree took three years to earn. Perhaps he planned on applying for another extension for the final year after he became settled in Padua. It is also possible that he had another reason to wish to study in Padua. The city was a center of a new type of study called humanism. This field is the belief that the search for true knowledge rested on active human endeavors. In any case, he was given the extension on his leave and took up medical training at the University of Padua. He completed only two years of medical studies at Padua, one year short of earning a medical degree. He then earned his doctorate in canon law from the University of Ferrara.

He returned to Lidzbark to stay at the house of his uncle, Bishop Watzenrode. His medical knowledge was sufficient for him to serve as personal physician to the bishop. And his canon law degree allowed him to serve in official positions in the church. However, his thoughts always returned to understanding the motions of the universe. Those thoughts eventually led him to challenge Ptolemy's geocentric universe and the church's official teachings.

MOVING HEAVEN AND EARTH

*U*nlike many pioneering thinkers whose ideas transformed science, Copernicus was anything but a rebel. After completing his formal education, he spent his entire career as an official of the Catholic Church. Yet even as he carried out his duties, an idea was growing in his mind that would eventually challenge Catholic doctrine, revolutionize science, and change the way that people viewed the place of Earth—and humanity—in the universe.

The more information astronomers gathered about the motion of the planets, the more complicated Ptolemy's model had to become in order to match what they were seeing. Copernicus struggled to find a simpler explanation. He was especially troubled by the need for the deferent and equant.

THIS SIXTEENTH-CENTURY PORTRAIT OF COPERNICUS AT ST. JOHN'S CHURCH IN TORUŃ IS PART OF A MEMORIAL DISPLAY THERE. IT CAPTURES BOTH THE RELIGIOUS AND SCIENTIFIC ASPECTS OF HIS LIFE. THE CRUCIFIX AND HIS PRAYERFUL POSE SHOW HIS SERVICE TO THE CATHOLIC CHURCH, WHILE A SHELF ON THE UPPER RIGHT HOLDS THE INSTRUMENTS ASTRONOMERS USED BEFORE THE INVENTION OF THE TELESCOPE.

NON PAREM PAVLO GRATIÃ· REQVIRO
VENIAM PETRI NEQ. POSCO, SED QVAM
IN CRVCIS LIGNO DEDERAS LATRONI
SEDVLVS ORO

No one knows exactly when he realized that describing the universe as heliocentric was the simplification he was looking for. But by 1514, he was confident enough in that idea to begin sharing it with a small number of trusted scholars in a document that later became known as his *Commentariolus* ("Little Commentary").

A POSITION OF TRUST

In Lidzbark in 1503, Copernicus gained the permission of the other chapter canons to carry out official church duties while also serving as the personal doctor of his uncle, Bishop Watzenrode. At that time, church officials were not just influential in religious matters. They were also politically powerful in their communities. This allowed the bishop to include Copernicus in important political matters. He served as his uncle's trusted adviser and confidant on numerous occasions.

When, in 1508, the pope granted Copernicus the right to two more offices that would provide him with income for little work, it seemed as if he was on course to become the hand-groomed successor to his aging uncle. But that was not to be: he never took the offices to which he was entitled. In 1510, he gave up his bonus as episcopal physician and left his uncle's side. He moved from Lidzbark back to the canon chapter headquarters in Frombork.

Why did Nicolaus Copernicus give up a promising chance at gaining a high office within the Catholic

COPERNICUS VS. PTOLEMY

Copernicus's *Commentariolus* did not eliminate all the complications in Ptolemy's description of the universe. His main simplification was the elimination of the deferents and equant. However, the path of the planets in the sky still could not be described by perfect circular motion at constant speed. Because the *Commentariolus* was merely a framework and not a complete mathematical description, the problem of epicycles remained. (In fact, Copernicus was never successful in addressing the need for non-circular orbits, even in *De Revolutionibus*.)

The *Commentariolus* may have contained its most revolutionary idea in a single word: "other." When Copernicus wrote that Earth revolves around the sun "like any other planet," he declared Earth to be not a unique body but rather one of six planets known at the time.

Church, with all of the influence, money, and prestige that went with it? No one knows for certain, but it was also around this time that many historians believe he began writing his *Commentariolus*.

COPERNICUS'S SEVEN PRINCIPLES

In the *Commentariolus*, Copernicus set down a basic framework for a heliocentric universe. Though its mathematics was not fully developed, the treatise laid out seven important principles. It was both revolution-ary and potentially dangerous to Copernicus's position as a canon. The thinking of Aristotle and Ptolemy had come to serve as the scientific basis for the church doctrine that Earth and humanity were at the center of everything.

If Copernicus was going to challenge the central-ity of Earth, he needed to have the support of other eminent scholars. Without that support, he would be risking serious criticism, ridicule, or even accusations of the crime of heresy. He put his thoughts down in writing and sent them to colleagues he respected and trusted, mainly those with whom he had studied in his early career at Kraków. He wrote them a letter detailing the seven principles that defined the motion of Earth and the planets, which he had developed through his research and thinking. As translated by Edward Rosen, an eminent historian of astronomy, the principles were:

1. There is no one center of all the celestial circles or spheres.
2. The center of Earth is not the center of the universe, but only of gravity and of the lunar sphere. (In other words, only the moon orbits Earth, not the sun or the planets.)
3. All the spheres revolve around the sun as the midpoint, and therefore the sun is the center of the universe.

THIS ARTISTIC REPRESENTATION IS A TRIBUTE TO COPERNICUS FOR HIS REVOLUTIONARY DESCRIPTION OF THE UNIVERSE AS HELIOCENTRIC. IT REFLECTS THE STATE OF KNOWLEDGE IN THE EARLY SEVENTEENTH CENTURY. THE SUN IS AT THE CENTER WITH THE ORBITS OF THE PLANETS GOING OUTWARD: MERCURY, VENUS, EARTH AND THE MOON, MARS, JUPITER WITH ITS FOUR GALILEAN MOONS, AND SATURN.

4. The ratio of Earth's distance from the sun to the height of the firmament (Copernicus's name for the location of the stars) is so much smaller than the ratio of Earth's radius to its distance from the sun that the distance from

Earth to the sun is imperceptible in comparison with the height of the firmament. (In other words, even though the stars orbit the sun, they are so far away that they seem to us to be rotating around Earth.)

5. Whatever motion appears in the firmament arises not from any motion of the firmament but from Earth's motion. Earth together with its circumjacent elements (air and water) performs a complete rotation on its fixed poles in a daily motion, while the firmament and highest heaven abide unchanged.

6. What appear to us as motions of the sun arise not from the sun's motion but from the motion of Earth and our sphere, with which it revolves around the sun like any other planet. Earth has, then, more than one motion.

7. The apparent retrograde and direct motion of the planets arises not from their motion but from Earth's. The motion of Earth alone, therefore, suffices to explain so many apparent inequalities in the heavens.

Using the knowledge that he had gained from years of observations, Copernicus described why these new ideas were true, and the ideas handed down from Ptolemy and the other ancient Greeks were not. While Copernicus did not give mathematical proofs in this first letter, he did say that he was thinking about them and would provide them in a later document. This showed that he planned to do further work on the problem.

After writing and distributing the *Commentariolus* to a limited audience, Copernicus quickly realized that many of the observations he was working with were ancient and possibly not very accurate. He needed better data to test the ideas that he put forth in the *Commentariolus*. It would take Copernicus nearly three decades to provide sufficient evidence to support his heliocentric system. He would reveal this evidence in his masterpiece, *De Revolutionibus Orbium Coelestium* ("On the Revolutions of the Heavenly Spheres").

CHAPTER FIVE

A REVOLUTIONARY BOOK

*B*ecause the *Commentariolus* was never published during Copernicus's lifetime, its value is more historical than scientific. It represents the beginning of a long process of observation and thinking that led to one of the greatest masterpieces of science, *De Revolutionibus Orbium Coelestium* ("On the Revolutions of the Heavenly Spheres"), commonly called *De Revolutionibus*. It would take almost the rest of Copernicus's seventy-year lifetime for this great book to be published.

STRUGGLES AND OBLIGATIONS

In 1512, Copernicus suffered a personal blow when his uncle, Bishop Watzenrode, died of

THIS MURAL IN THE CATHEDRAL OF KWIDZYN IN NORTHERN POLAND DEPICTS THREE LEADERS OF THE ORDER OF TEUTONIC KNIGHTS, WHO BATTLED TO TAKE OVER THE PART OF POLAND WHERE COPERNICUS LIVED BETWEEN 1519 AND 1521. COPERNICUS BECAME A LEADER OF THE RESISTANCE TO THE ORDER AFTER A FIRE BURNED HIS RESIDENCE TO THE GROUND AND FORCED HIM TO FLEE TO A NEARBY CASTLE, WHERE HE REMAINED UNTIL A 1521 PEACE TREATY.

illness. Even though he had left Lidzbark and was no longer working directly with the bishop, this must have been a painful loss for Nicolaus. His uncle had looked out for him since age ten after the death of his father.

Even without his uncle's powerful influence, the other church leaders recognized Copernicus's brilliance and skills. This led to important duties that often forced his passion for astronomy into the background. For example, the other canons of his chapter selected him to be the administrator, a position in which he had to concentrate on managing the lands the chapter owned. It was a wise choice for the church. His duties required him to think about matters related to the value of money, and he eventually published four books on the subject.

He also found himself in the middle of a political and military conflict. From 1519 to 1521, the Order of Teutonic Knights again tried to gain control over a large part of the kingdom of Poland. Fierce fighting swirled around the area where Copernicus lived. At one point, the buildings where he lived burned to the ground, and Copernicus was forced to flee to a nearby castle. He became a leader in the resistance to the knights until a peace treaty was signed in 1521.

CREATING A MASTERPIECE

Despite these distractions, Copernicus continued to develop the themes of the *Commentariolus*. He continued to observe the sun, planets, and stars. He even developed a new instrument called a solar table to record more information about the location of the sun in the sky. The device was simply a mirror that reflected sunlight onto a wall. On the wall he had marked lines that represented an imaginary equator for the universe. By seeing where the sun hit these marks, Copernicus was able to better determine the time until the next equinox, one of two points in the year when the lengths of day and night are equal.

This tool and others provided him with the observations he needed to refine his ideas. He began to write a book that became *De Revolutionibus*. *De Revolutionibus* described a heliocentric universe. Copernicus set Earth turning on its axis and rearranged the heavenly order so that the moon orbited Earth and the planets (including Earth) orbited the sun, which was at the center of the universe. The book included new data in the form of tables and charts developed from his years of astronomical observations.

The key sections of the book were comparisons between his heliocentric model of the universe and Ptolemy's geocentric one. Mathematically, he showed that it was no longer necessary to include the deferent and equant to understand the motion of the heavenly bodies. But he did need to add the fact that Earth was spinning around its axis once a day. He kept Ptolemy's idea about the perfectly circular nature of the heavenly bodies' orbits. That required him to include some epicycles. By putting Earth in orbit around the sun, however, his description of the universe needed many fewer of them than Ptolemy's did.

Historians of astronomy believe that *De Revolutionibus* took about twenty-six years to complete. While the exact date is not certain, most of them agree that it was begun sometime in 1515. By 1530, most of the work had been set down, but after spending all this time and effort, Copernicus did not feel that he could share his great masterpiece yet.

Rheticus, a young astronomer who came to study with Copernicus in 1539, persuaded him that this great work should be published. In 1540, Rheticus published a short description, called the *Narratio Prima* ("First Narration"), of what Copernicus planned to release. This work was designed to generate interest in Copernicus's book and to see what controversy would be generated by the idea that Earth is not the center of the universe but merely one of the sun's six planets. The reaction among the scholarly community seemed favorable, so Rheticus urged Copernicus to go on with his plans. By September 1541, Copernicus had finished his manuscript and sent it off to Nuremberg, Germany, to have it printed.

THE STRUCTURE OF *DE REVOLUTIONIBUS*

Copernicus structured *De Revolutionibus* as six sections, or "books," with each further divided into chapters. The opening chapters in each book were a basic description of the idea and argument that Copernicus was going to make. The following chapters demonstrated the strength of those arguments using geometry and included charts of his astronomical observations as

AMERICAN ANTIQUE BOOKSELLER JONATHAN HILL DISPLAYS THE DIAGRAM OF THE HELIOCENTRIC UNIVERSE IN A RARE FIRST EDITION OF VOLUME SIX OF NICOLAUS COPERNICUS'S *DE REVOLUTIONIBUS ORBIUM COELESTIUM*, PUBLISHED IN 1543, AT THE 2008 TOKYO INTERNATIONAL ANTIQUE BOOK FAIR.

supporting data. By building up his arguments in such a logical manner, Copernicus believed that he could persuade others that the book's revolutionary proposition, set out in *De Revolutionibus*'s preface, was valid. The earth moved around its own axis, while orbiting a sun located at the center of the universe.

In the first section of *De Revolutionibus*, he set out the parts of prior astronomical learning that he found to be true—namely, that all planetary motion was in the shape of a circle. He also agreed that ancient authorities were correct when they said that the universe was composed of interconnected spheres that held the sun, planets, stars, and Earth. He then wrote why and how he disagreed with thinkers like Ptolemy, Plato, and others that Earth did not move.

Copernicus also included a dramatic item that he must have known would draw attention to his work: he drew a new map of the heavens. It showed the sun sitting in the middle of the universe surrounded by the spheres of the planets. First Mercury and then Venus circled the sun. Next came Earth with the moon orbiting it and then Mars, Jupiter, and Saturn. Finally came the sphere holding the stars. For the first time, people could see in print that Earth no longer held the primary place in the universe but was just another planet like the others.

In the second section of *De Revolutionibus*, Copernicus described the geometry of circles that he believed would persuade readers to accept this radical change from previous thinking. In the third and fourth sections of *De Revolutionibus*, he showed how his idea predicted Earth's equinoxes and solstices more accurately.

In the last two sections, he provided his mathematical descriptions of the motions of the five planets through the sky, again with greater accuracy than there had been in the past. Throughout the book, he provided tables of observations that he had made during his long career. That enabled other scholars to confirm his reasoning. He believed that linking his thorough mathematical analysis and careful reasoning to the data would win them over. Their support would be particularly important, since *De Revolutionibus* challenged church doctrine about the position of Earth and humanity in the universe.

For that reason, Copernicus remained worried that religious authorities, especially Pope Paul III, might condemn him for the contents of his book. In an effort to gain the favor of the Catholic Church, he wrote a special preface and dedication to the pope to be included with the book's main body. In this preface, Copernicus acknowledged that some would attack him for what he had written, but that he had published his book to help the church produce a more accurate calendar to precisely mark holy days such as Easter.

Copernicus hoped this practical application would keep *De Revolutionibus* from being denounced by those in the church who thought it was blasphemous. Unfortunately, he did not need to worry about such matters for long. His book was published sometime at the end of March 1543, about two months before his death on May 24. Despite the many legends that have spread throughout the centuries, he most likely never saw a copy of his finished printed work.

THE RISKS OF CHALLENGING CHURCH DOCTRINE

Copernicus was well aware that challenging church doctrine could lead to great problems. In 1517, not long after he began compiling the data that would support his ideas in *De Revolutionibus*, a Catholic priest named Martin Luther wrote a list of ninety-five theses, or arguments about things that he thought the Catholic Church needed to fix. It is believed that he nailed the list to the door of a church in Wittenberg, Germany. The contents were so divisive that the Catholic Church eventually expelled Luther as a heretic. However, Luther had gained so many followers all across western Europe that when he was forced out, they decided to follow him and form a new church. This would be the start of series of breaks, which became known as the Protestant Reformation, that would slowly erode the Catholic Church's power in politics, culture, and religion throughout western Europe.

DE REVOLUTIONIBUS REVOLUTIONIZES ASTRONOMY

In the years following the publication of *De Revolutionibus*, Copernicus's great book set in motion many new ideas in astronomy. But as he had feared, at first most religious leaders considered it heresy and a direct threat to Scripture. This occurred despite Copernicus's attempts to win the pope's favor and his student Rheticus's similar attempts to gain the approval of Martin Luther and the leaders of the Reformation.

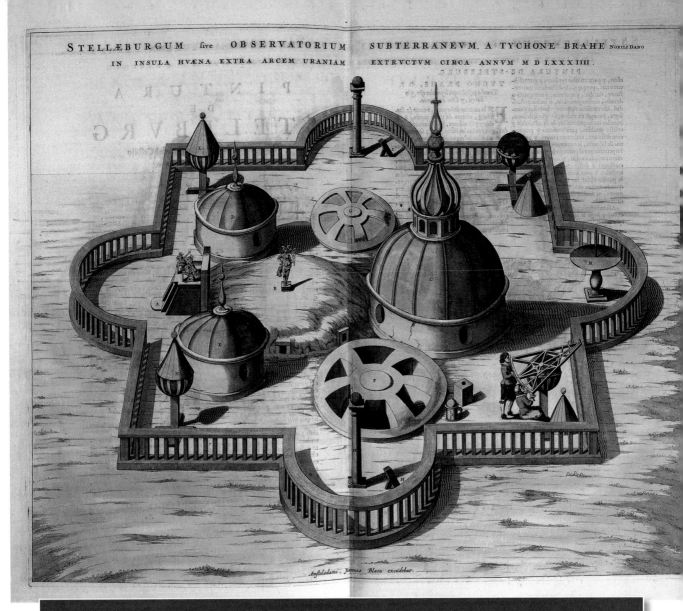

STELLÆBURGUM five OBSERVATORIUM SUBTERRANEUM, A TYCHONE BRAHE NOBILI DANO IN INSULA HVÆNA EXTRA ARCEM URANIAM EXTRVCTVM CIRCA ANNVM M D LXXXIIII.

THIS REPRODUCTION OF A 1584 DRAWING SHOWS HOW TYCHO BRAHE'S GREAT OBSERVATORY WAS LAID OUT. THE TWO ASTRONOMERS IN THE LOWER RIGHT APPEAR TO BE TRACKING THE POSITION OF THE SUN.

Astronomers, however, could not ignore *De Revolutionibus* because of the detailed mathematical analysis and charts that Copernicus had included to support his conclusions. European royalty also took notice. For example, the king of Denmark employed the great

Danish astronomer Tycho Brahe (1546–1601) to investigate and evaluate Copernicus's work. In order to do this, Brahe realized that he, too, would need to spend years making accurate astronomical observations. He improved on the existing instruments needed to make these observations and built what is now considered the first true astronomical observatory.

Brahe's religious convictions did not allow him to accept Copernicus's heliocentric system, but he could not refute it without data. Years later, his assistant, Johannes Kepler (1571–1630), used rigorous astronomical observations not only to support Copernicus's system but also to improve on it in a way that eliminated the need for epicycles altogether. Kepler figured out that Earth and the other planets did not move in perfectly circular paths around the sun but rather followed oval paths called ellipses. That turned out to be the first of three laws of orbital motion that he discovered and are still used in astronomy today.

GALILEO GALILEI, THE TELESCOPE, AND THE BODIES OF THE SOLAR SYSTEM

Galileo Galilei (1564–1642) was another scientist who took the ideas of Copernicus as the basis for his own work. In 1609, Galileo refined a new invention called the telescope and turned it heavenward. He saw mountains on the moon, showing that it was definitely another world. He discovered that Venus exhibited phases like the moon, which meant it had to be closer to the sun than Earth.

But perhaps his most dramatic discovery was four points of light in a line around Jupiter. Observing them over several nights, he noticed them moving from one side of Jupiter to the other. He realized that they were moons in orbit around Jupiter. They were the first heavenly bodies whose motion was definitely not around Earth. After that, people found

REPRESENTATIVES OF THE MUSEO GALILEO IN FLORENCE, ITALY, CAREFULLY PREPARE A 3-FOOT-LONG (91 CM) TELESCOPE USED BY GALILEO GALILEI FOR DISPLAY AT THE FRANKLIN INSTITUTE IN PHILADELPHIA, PENNSYLVANIA, ON APRIL 1, 2009. IN 1610, GALILEO DISCOVERED FOUR MOONS ORBITING JUPITER, PROVIDING EVIDENCE THAT NOT ALL BODIES IN THE SKY REVOLVED AROUND EARTH.

it much easier to give up Ptolemy's geocentric system and replace it with a heliocentric one.

Even so, nearly 150 years after the Catholic Church rejected Copernicus's ideas and punished people who declared them to be true, Galileo shared a similar fate. He, too, was condemned by the Catholic Church, and he died while under house arrest.

COUNTING THE PLANETS

The discovery of Uranus in 1781 as the seventh planet seemed to confirm a mathematical pattern in planetary distances called the Titius-Bode law. However, there was a gap between the orbits of Mars and Jupiter. In 1801 and 1802, astronomers spotted two more objects, Ceres and Pallas, just about the right distance from the sun to fill that gap. Then in 1804 and 1807, they discovered two more bodies, Juno and Vesta. That brought the number of planets up to eleven, though astronomer William Herschel suggested that the newer bodies should be called "asteroids." When several new asteroids were discovered beginning in 1845, astronomers stopped calling asteroids planets. After that decision and the discovery of Neptune in 1846, the number of planets was set at eight. We now know of thousands of asteroids, with more being discovered regularly.

After several years of observations of Neptune, astronomers found irregularities in its orbit that they couldn't account for by considering the strong gravity of Uranus, Saturn, and Jupiter. The search began for another planet farther out, and it led to the discovery of Pluto in 1931. The count of planets was back to nine. However, as scientists studied Pluto, they discovered that it was too small

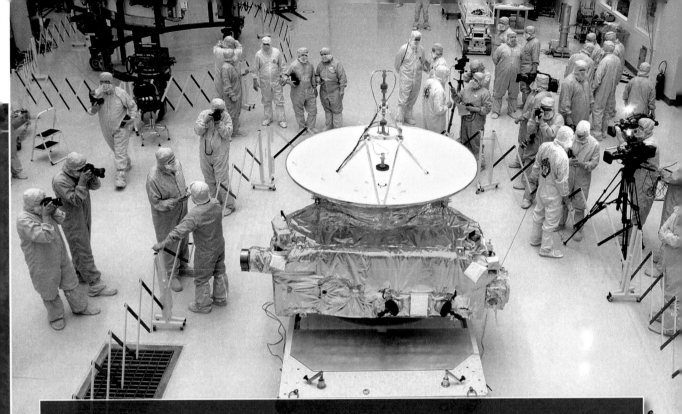

IN NOVEMBER 2005, WRITERS, PHOTOGRAPHERS, AND JOURNALISTS WEARING PROTECTIVE CLOTHING WERE GIVEN AN OPPORTUNITY TO VIEW THE *NEW HORIZONS* SPACECRAFT IN ITS PREPARATION AREA AT THE KENNEDY SPACE CENTER IN FLORIDA. IN JANUARY 2006, IT WAS LAUNCHED TOWARD PLUTO AND THE KUIPER BELT, WHERE IT IS EXPECTED TO ARRIVE IN 2015.

to account for the irregularities in Neptune's path. Then in the late 1970s, two *Voyager* spacecraft traveling past Jupiter, Saturn, Uranus, and Neptune produced better measurements of their masses, and that solved the problem. Neptune's orbit was well behaved, and a large planet farther out wasn't needed after all.

Since then other bodies like Pluto, including one of comparable size called Eris, have been discovered in a region of the solar system called the Kuiper Belt. In 2006, the International Astronomical Union (IAU) wrote a definition of the term "major planet" that ruled out Pluto. But that doesn't make it any less interesting. A spacecraft named *New Horizons* launched not long before the IAU vote is expected to reach the Kuiper Belt in 2015. Pluto and its moons will be *New Horizon*'s first target for study.

Over the years, knowledge of the solar system grew, including Sir William Herschel's discovery of the planet Uranus in 1781. Even more remarkable was the 1846 discovery of Neptune. Astronomers had noticed deviations of Uranus's motion from its predicted orbit and suspected that it was experiencing the gravitational influence of another planet. Mathematicians calculated where that planet might be found, and astronomers in the Berlin Observatory spotted it very close to its predicted position.

With the discovery of Uranus and Neptune, it was no longer possible for critics to deny the truth of the work of Galileo, Kepler, and Isaac Newton, and the foundation upon which it was built—the heliocentric universe of Nicolaus Copernicus.

THE CHANGING CENTER OF THE UNIVERSE

Aristarchus was the first scholar to replace Earth with the sun at the center of the universe, and Copernicus probably had read Aristarchus's writings. So why is Copernicus considered a revolutionary thinker? The answer lies in *De Revolutionibus*. The measurements of the ancients were simply not accurate and detailed enough to develop a clear preference for a heliocentric system over a geocentric system. It took Copernicus's

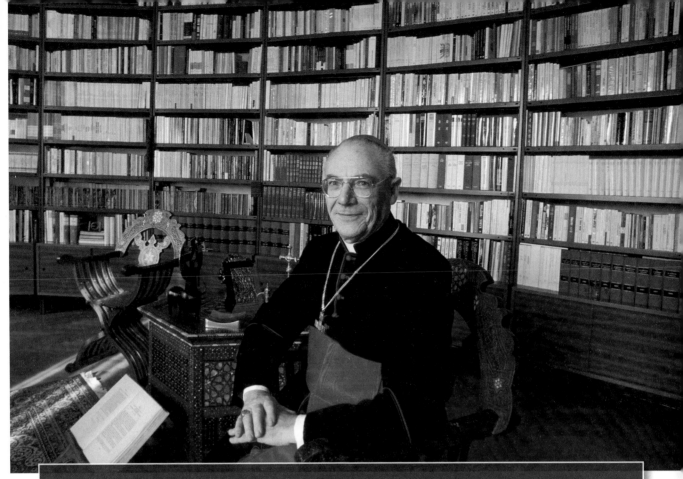

ROMAN CATHOLIC CARDINAL PAUL POUPARD LED THE RESEARCH TEAM THAT PROVIDED THE EVIDENCE FOR THE CHURCH'S 1992 REVERSAL OF ITS 1633 CONVICTION OF GALILEO FOR HERESY.

years of careful measurements and thoughtful analysis to produce the tables and persuasive arguments in that masterpiece.

But even then, the church and most of society rejected the idea of a heliocentric universe. It conflicted with everyday experience and especially the church's interpretation of the Bible, which made humanity the focus of God's attention. Eventually, thanks largely to Kepler's laws and Galileo's observations, the idea of a sun-centered universe became more acceptable. Even as the church confined Galileo to house arrest, it accepted the heliocentric theory as a useful calculating device.

In 1687, Sir Isaac Newton published a theory of gravity that explained why Kepler's laws were correct, but until the middle of the eighteenth century the church continued to reject the idea that anything other than Earth was at the center of the universe. It banned heliocentric books until 1758, and it did not approve of the printing of heliocentric books in Rome until 1822. It was not until 1992 that the church finally admitted that it had been in error and reversed the decisions of Galileo's tribunal.

By then, science had made remarkable strides

COPERNICUS'S IDEAS MOVED HEAVEN AND EARTH AND TRANSFORMED HUMANITY'S VIEW OF OUR PLANET'S PLACE IN THE UNIVERSE. WE NOW KNOW THAT OUR WORLD DOES NOT HAVE TO BE IN THE CENTER OF EVERYTHING TO BE AN IMPORTANT CENTER OF KNOWLEDGE AND DISCOVERY.

that changed the very meaning of "center of the universe." First, astronomers recognized that the sun was not the center of the universe but just one star of many. Then came the discovery of galaxies. At that point, scientists realized that the sun was located far from the center of a typical galaxy called the Milky Way. Our galaxy contains many billions of stars, perhaps as many as a trillion, and we are now discovering that a large number of those stars have solar systems like our own. We also know that there are trillions of similar galaxies in the visible universe.

And where is the center of that universe? According to Albert Einstein's 1905 theory of relativity, that question has no answer. The position and motion of any object can only be measured relative to another object. It can't be measured absolutely. Having a center would provide a way to measure absolute motion in violation of Einstein's discovery.

To some people, that makes Earth seem very unimportant. But there is a better way to look at things. Our planet is the center of life as we know it, and like Nicolaus Copernicus, each of us can live a life of discovery and play an important part in its future.

TIMELINE

FEBRUARY 19, 1473 Nicolaus Copernicus is born.

1483 Copernicus's father dies, leaving his education in the hands of his uncle.

1492–1494 Copernicus pursues undergraduate studies at Kraków, where he likely learns astronomical observation skills.

1496–1499 Copernicus enrolls in Bologna and studies with the innovative astronomer da Novara, who challenged some of Ptolemy's work.

MARCH 9, 1497 In his first recorded celestial observation, Copernicus (along with da Novara) notes that the moon passed in front of the star Aldebaran.

C. 1514 Copernicus circulates his *Commentariolus* ("Little Commentary"), in which he first proposes a sun-centered universe, to trusted scholars.

C. 1530 Copernicus completes his major work on the heliocentric theory of planetary motion.

1539 Rheticus comes to study with Copernicus and encourages him to publish the book that became *De Revolutionibus Orbium Coelestium* ("On the Revolutions of the Heavenly Spheres").

MARCH 1543 *De Revolutionibus* is published.

MAY 24, 1543 Copernicus dies in Frombork, Poland.

1609 Johannes Kepler publishes his first two laws of planetary motion. Kepler agrees with Copernicus that Earth is a planet that orbits the sun like the other known planets.

1610 Galileo Galilei observes four moons orbiting Jupiter, showing that not all heavenly motion is around Earth.

1619 Kepler publishes a textbook that includes his third law of planetary motion. The law relates the orbital periods of planets to their distance from the sun. Since the length of Earth's year and its distance from the sun obey the relationship, the third law strengthens the idea of a heliocentric universe.

1781 Sir William Herschel discovers Uranus.

1801–1807 Astronomers discover the first four asteroids, Ceres, Pallas, Juno, and Vesta.

1846 Astronomers at the Berlin Observatory discover Neptune.

1930 Clyde Tombaugh of the Lowell Observatory discovers Pluto.

1977 Two *Voyager* spacecraft are launched on fly-by missions to Jupiter, Saturn, Uranus, and Neptune.

2006 The *New Horizons* spacecraft is launched toward Pluto and the Kuiper Belt for 2015 arrival.

2013 The *New Horizons* spacecraft reaches the halfway point between orbits of Uranus and Neptune.

2015 The *New Horizons* spacecraft is expected to fly by Pluto.

GLOSSARY

AXIS A straight line on which an object turns or seems to turn.

CANON An official who administers the business of a cathedral.

CANON LAW The official laws of a church.

DEFERENT A circle centered on the point halfway between Earth and the equant, used to show a planet's main motion in Ptolemy's geocentric description of the universe.

EPICYCLE A circle around a point on the deferent, used to explain the paths of the sun, moon, and planets in Ptolemy's geocentric description of the universe.

EQUANT A point in Ptolemy's geocentric description of the universe, used to explain the sun's changing speed around Earth at different times of the year. Ptolemy stated that the sun changed the angle it made with the line between the equant and Earth at a constant rate.

EQUATOR A circle running in an east-west direction along the center of a sphere or a spherical body like a planet, separating it into two equal halves.

EQUINOX One of the two days of the year when both night and day are of equal length all over the world. An equinox marks the beginning of the spring and fall seasons.

GALAXY A system of billions of stars.

GEOCENTRIC A description of the universe that places Earth in its center.

HELIOCENTRIC A description of the universe that places the sun in its center.

HERESY Belief or opinion contrary to religious doctrine.

HERETIC One who dissents, or refuses to accept, accepted beliefs or standards.

HUMANISM A school of learning that believes that the work produced by humankind is worth studying.

LATITUDE The distance north or south of the equator, measured by degrees.

MERCHANT A person who buys and sells goods.

MIDDLE AGES A period in European history following the fall of the Roman Empire in 476 CE and continuing through approximately the late fourteenth century, during which progress in art, science, and scholarship slowed or declined.

REFORMATION A period in Christian history during which religious reformers such as Martin Luther challenged the Roman Catholic Church and ultimately produced new Protestant churches under their leadership.

RENAISSANCE A period in European history from the fourteenth to seventeenth centuries when progress in art, science, and scholarship flourished.

FOR MORE INFORMATION

American Astronomical Society (AAS)

2000 Florida Avenue NW, Suite 400

Washington, DC 20009

(202) 328-2010

Web site: http://www.aas.org

The mission of the AAS is to enhance and share humanity's scientific understanding of the universe. In addition to sponsoring meetings and publishing journals for scientists, it publishes information for the public, educators, and people interested in careers in astronomy.

American Institute of Physics (AIP)

One Physics Ellipse

College Park, MD 20740-3843

(301) 209-3100

Web site: http://www.aip.org

The AIP is the umbrella organization for many different professional societies of physical scientists. It publishes numerous journals for scientists and magazines for educators, the public, and students interested in careers in physics. Its Center for the History of Physics contains a library and archive of historical books and photographs related to the history of science. Online articles and images are available as well.

Nicolaus Copernicus House Museum

ul. Kopernika 15/17

87-100 Toruń

Poland

Web sites: http://www.visittorun.pl/365,l2.html#
copernicushouse

This museum consists of two homes that were owned
by Copernicus's father after he moved to Toruń.
The larger one was built around 1350, and the
smaller dates back to 1464–1480. The museum
houses numerous permanent exhibits that capture
the history of Toruń, as well as Copernicus's work
and the culture in which he lived.

Nicolaus Copernicus Museum in Frombork

ul. Katedralna 8

14-530 Frombork

Poland

Web site: http://www.frombork.art.pl

Located on the grounds of the former bishop's palace in
Frombork, where Copernicus spent much of his career as a canon in the Roman Catholic Church, the
museum houses a planetarium and numerous permanent exhibits about Copernicus's life and work
in both church affairs and astronomy. It also houses
historical and cultural exhibits about Frombork.

The Planetary Society

85 South Grand Avenue

Pasadena, CA 91105

(626) 793-5100

Web site: http://www.planetary.org

Founded in 1980 by Carl Sagan, Bruce Murray, and Louis Friedman, the Planetary Society aims to inspire and involve the public in space exploration through advocacy, projects, and education. The organization's chief executive officer is Bill Nye the Science Guy.

Royal Astronomical Society of Canada (RASC)

203-4920 Dundas Street W

Toronto, ON M9A 1B7

Canada

(888) 924-7272

Web site: http://www.rasc.ca

The Royal Astronomical Society of Canada is Canada's leading astronomy organization. It aims to inspire curiosity about the universe, share scientific knowledge, and foster understanding of astronomy through activities including education, research, and community outreach. Its publications and its extensive Web site have materials for scientists, researchers, teachers, and students of all ages.

WEB SITES

Due to the changing nature of Internet links, Rosen Publishing has developed an online list of Web sites related to the subject of this book. This site is updated regularly. Please use this link to access the list:

http://www.rosenlinks.com/RDSP/coper

FOR FURTHER READING

Anderson, Michael. *Pioneers in Astronomy and Space Exploration* (Inventors and Innovators). New York, NY: Britannica Educational Publishing in association with Rosen Educational Services, 2013.

Bell, Trudy E. *Earth's Journey Through Space* (Scientific American). New York, NY: Chelsea House, 2008.

Bortz, Fred. *Seven Wonders of Exploration Technology*. Minneapolis, MN: Twenty-First Century Books, 2010.

Bortz, Fred. *Seven Wonders of Space Technology*. Minneapolis, MN: Twenty-First Century Books, 2011.

Carson, Mary Kay. *Beyond the Solar System: Exploring Galaxies, Black Holes, Alien Planets, and More: A History with 21 Activities*. Chicago, IL: Chicago Review Press, 2013.

Dyson, Marianne J. *Astronomy: Decade by Decade* (Twentieth-Century Science). New York, NY: Facts On File, 2007.

Karam, P. Andrew, and Ben P. Stein. *Planetary Motion* (Science Foundations). New York, NY: Chelsea House, 2009.

Mazer, Arthur. *Shifting the Earth: The Mathematical Quest to Understand the Motion of the Universe*. Hoboken, NJ: Wiley, 2011.

Miller, Ron. *Recentering the Universe: The Radical Theories of Copernicus, Kepler, and Galileo*. Minneapolis, MN: Twenty-First Century Books, 2014.

Repcheck, Jack. *Copernicus' Secret: How the Scientific Revolution Began.* New York, NY: Simon & Schuster, 2007.

Robinson, Andrew, ed. *The Scientists: An Epic of Discovery.* New York, NY: Thames and Hudson, 2012.

Sobel, Dava. *A More Perfect Heaven: How Copernicus Revolutionized the Cosmos.* New York, NY: Walker, 2011.

Somervill, Barbara A. *Nicolaus Copernicus: Father of Modern Astronomy* (Signature Lives). Minneapolis, MN: Capstone, 2008.

Timmons, Todd. *Makers of Western Science: The Works and Words of 24 Visionaries from Copernicus to Watson and Crick.* Jefferson, NC: McFarland & Co., 2012.

Tyson, Neil deGrasse. *The Pluto Files: The Rise and Fall of America's Favorite Planet.* New York, NY: Norton, 2009.

Vollmann, William T. *Uncentering the Earth: Copernicus and the Revolutions of the Heavenly Spheres.* New York, NY: W. W. Norton, 2007.

BIBLIOGRAPHY

Andronik, Catherine M. *Copernicus: Founder of Modern Astronomy* (Great Minds of Science). Berkeley Heights, NJ: Enslow, 2002.

Bortz, Fred. *Physics: Decade by Decade* (Twentieth-Century Science). New York, NY: Facts On File, 2007.

Copernicus, Nicolaus, and Edward Rosen. *On the Revolutions.* Baltimore, MD: Johns Hopkins University Press, 1992.

Copernicus, Nicolaus, Georg Joachim Rheticus, and Edward Rosen. *Three Copernican Treatises: The Commentariolus of Copernicus, The Letter Against Werner, The Narratio Prima of Rheticus.* New York, NY: Columbia University Press, 1939.

Cropper, William H. *Great Physicists: The Life and Times of Leading Physicists from Galileo to Hawking.* New York, NY: Oxford University Press, 2001.

Dobrzycki, Jerzy, and International Union of the History and Philosophy of Science. *The Reception of Copernicus' Heliocentric Theory: Proceedings of a Symposium Organized by the Nicolas Copernicus Committee of the International Union of the History and Philosophy of Science, Toruń, Poland, 1973.* Boston, MA: D. Reidel Publishing Company, 1972.

Kuhn, T. S. *The Copernican Revolution: Planetary Astronomy in the Development of Western Thought.* Cambridge, MA: Harvard University Press, 1957.

McMullin, Ernan. *The Church and Galileo.* Notre Dame, IN: University of Notre Dame Press, 2005.

Rabin, Sheila. "Nicolaus Copernicus." *Stanford Encyclopedia of Philosophy*, 2010. Retrieved December 26, 2012 (http://plato.stanford.edu/archives/fall2010/entries/copernicus).

Ridpath, Ian, ed. *Oxford Dictionary of Astronomy*. 2nd ed. Oxford, England: Oxford University Press, 2007.

Rosen, Edward. *Copernicus and His Successors*. London, England: Hambledon Press, 1995.

Rosen, Edward. *Copernicus and the Scientific Revolution*. Malabar, FL: Krieger, 1984.

Sobel, Dava. *The Planets*. New York, NY: Viking, 2005.

Standage, Tom. *The Neptune File: A Story of Astronomical Rivalry and the Pioneers of Planet Hunting*. New York, NY: Walker, 2000.

Weisstein, Eric. W. "Copernicus, Nicholaus (1473–1543)." Eric Weisstein's World of Scientific Biography, Wolfram Research, 2007. Retrieved December 26, 2012 (http://scienceworld.wolfram.com/biography/Copernicus.html).

INDEX

A

Anaxagoras, 19, 20, 21
Aristarchus of Samos, 6, 26–27, 37, 62
Aristotle, 17, 21, 23, 24, 26, 27, 44
astronomy, ancient/early, 10–11, 16–29

B

Bologna, Italy, 30–32
Brahe, Tycho, 58

C

Catholic Church, 7, 12, 15, 25, 26, 27, 28, 29, 33, 36, 40, 44, 49–50, 55, 56, 60, 63, 64
Commentariolus, 42, 43–47, 48, 50
Copernicus, Andrew (brother), 31, 34–35, 36, 38
Copernicus, Nicolaus
  childhood of, 8, 12
  and the church, 15, 25, 27, 29, 33, 40, 42–43, 44, 49–50, 55, 56, 60
  education of, 12–15, 16, 30–33, 38–39
  and heliocentric theory, 38, 42, 43–47, 51, 52, 53, 60, 62–63
  importance of, 7
  invention of solar table, 50–51
  starts to challenge long-held beliefs, 33, 34, 37, 39
  study of ancient Greek, 37

D

da Novara, Domenico Maria, 32–33, 34
De Revolutionibus Orbium Coelestium, 34, 43, 47, 48, 51–52, 62
  importance of, 56–58
  structure of, 52–55

E

eclipses, early theories on, 20–21
Einstein, Albert, 65
Eudoxus, 17, 22–23

G

Galileo Galilei, 58–59, 62, 63–64
geocentric/Earth-centered universe, theory of, 6–7, 19, 24, 26, 27, 39, 40, 43, 51, 60, 62

H

heliocentric/sun-centered universe, theory of, 6, 26–27, 38, 42, 51, 52, 53, 60, 62–64
Herschel, William, 60, 62
humanism, 39

ABOUT THE AUTHOR

After earning his Ph.D. at Carnegie Mellon University in 1971, physicist Fred Bortz set off on an interesting and varied twenty-five-year career in teaching and research. From 1979 to 1994, he was on staff at Carnegie Mellon, where his work evolved from research to outreach.

After his third book, *Catastrophe! Great Engineering Failure—and Success*, was designated a "Selector's Choice" on the 1996 list of Outstanding Science Trade Books for Children, he decided to spend the rest of his career as a full-time writer. His books, now numbering nearly thirty, have since won awards, including the American Institute of Physics Science Writing Award, and recognition on several best books lists.

Known on the Internet as the smiling, bowtie-wearing "Dr. Fred," he welcomes inquisitive visitors to his Web site at http://www.fredbortz.com.

PHOTO CREDITS

Cover (portrait) Imagno/Hulton Fine Art Collection/Getty Images, (sphere) © iStockphotos.com/Ben Taylor; pp. 5, 18, 31, 64 iStockphoto/Thinkstock; p. 9 John Hay/Lonely Planet Images/Getty Images; p. 10 Leemage/Universal Images Group/Getty Images; p. 13 The Bridgeman Art Library/Getty Images; p. 20 AFP/Getty Images; p. 24 Wikimedia Commons; p. 26 Library of Congress Prints & Photographs Division; p. 33 MOF/E+/Getty Images; p. 35 © Mary Evans Picture Library/The Image Works; pp. 37, 45 DEA/J. E. Bulloz/De Agostini/Getty Images; p. 41 Erich Lessing/Art Resource, NY; p. 49 Wojtek Radwanski/AFP/Getty Images; p. 53 Yoshikazu Tsuno/AFP/Getty Images; p. 57 DEA/G. Dagli Orti/ De Agostini/Getty Images; p. 59 Tim Shaffer/Reuters/Landov; p. 61 Bruce Weaver/AFP/Getty Images; p. 63 Raphael Gaillarde/Gamma-Rapho/Getty Images; cover and interior pages (textured background) © iStockphoto.com/Perry Kroll, (atom illustrations) © iStockphoto.com/suprun.

Designer: Nicole Russo; Editor: Andrea Sclarow Paskoff; Photo Researcher: Amy Feinberg